The BOO

# PIANO
## ANTHOLOGY

33 pieces by 23 composers

BOOSEY & HAWKES

AN IMAGEM COMPANY

DISTRIBUTED BY

HAL•LEONARD®
CORPORATION
7777 W. BLUEMOUND RD. P.O. BOX 13819 MILWAUKEE, WI 53213

www.boosey.com
www.halleonard.com

# CONTENTS

* First edition, previously unpublished

# Image de Moreau
## Toccata

LOUIS ANDRIESSEN
(1999)

Almost completely without 🎵 until m. 153; no accents on the beat

il canto forte e legato

10

*for Carolyn Brunelle*

# Intermezzo

DOMINICK ARGENTO
(2010)

Andante ma molto rubato (♪= 138 ca.)

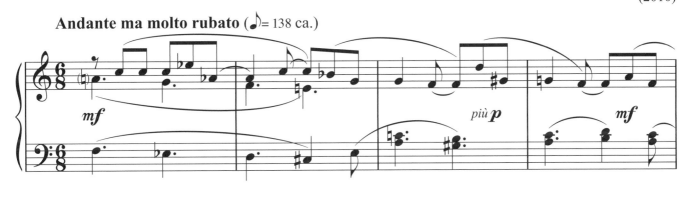

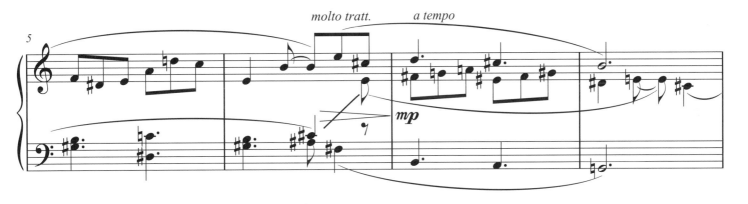

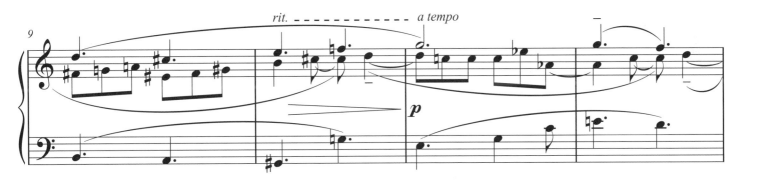

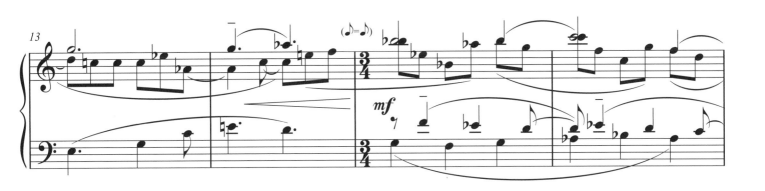

Christmas Day, 2010

# A Fugue in Flight

JACK BEESON
(2009)

poco rallentando al fine

number of repetitions
optional

# Seven Anniversaries

LEONARD BERNSTEIN
(1943)

## I. For Aaron Copland
(Nov. 14, 1900)

## II. For My Sister, Shirley
(Oct. 3, 1923)

### III. In Memoriam: Alfred Eisner
(Jan. 4, 1941)

**Andante serioso, un poco rubato** (♪ = 50)

## IV. For Paul Bowles
(Dec. 31, 1910)

## V. In Memoriam: Nathalie Koussevitzky
### (Jan. 15, 1942)

## VI. For Sergei Koussevitzky
(July 26, 1874)

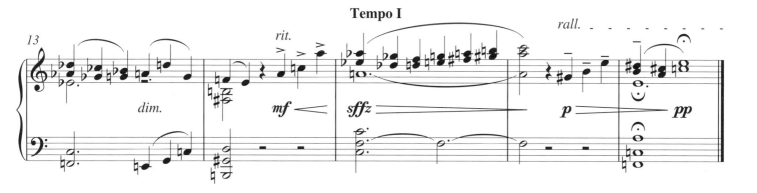

## VII. For William Schuman
(Aug. 4, 1910)

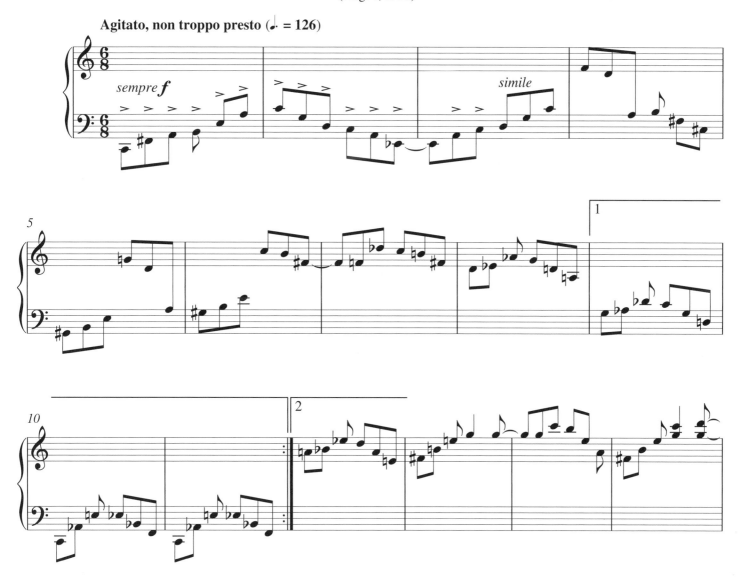

**Più mosso**

Boston - New York City
1942–43

# Night-Piece
## (Notturno)

BENJAMIN BRITTEN
(1963)

30

*These notes should be silently pressed
down before the pedal is released.

# Rosemary

from *Three Sketches*

FRANK BRIDGE
(1906)

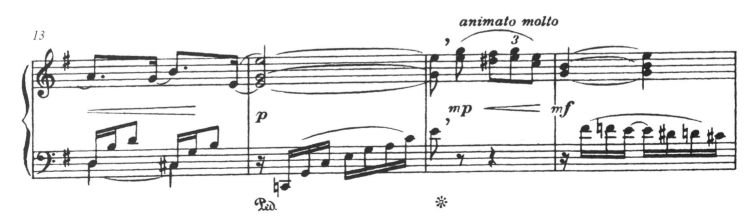

# Farewell to Stromness

from *The Yellow Cake Revue*

PETER MAXWELL DAVIES
(1980)

# Two Diversions

I

ELLIOTT CARTER
(1999)

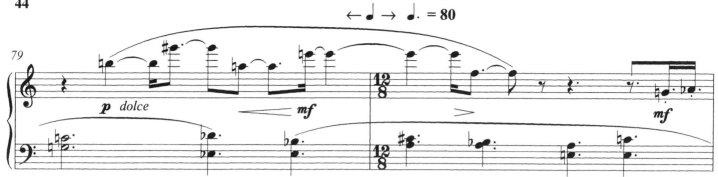

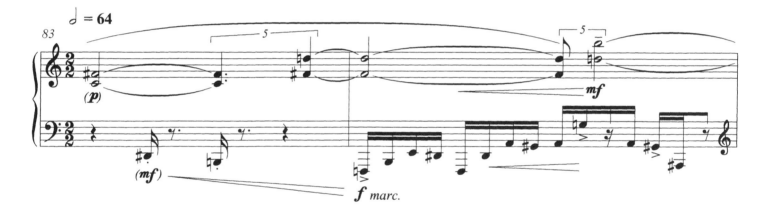

## II

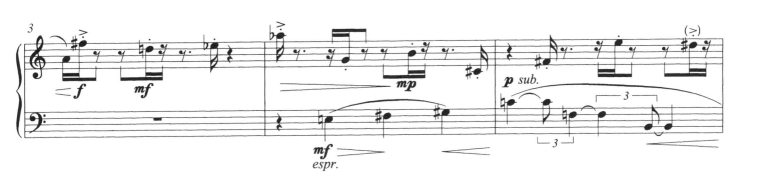

48

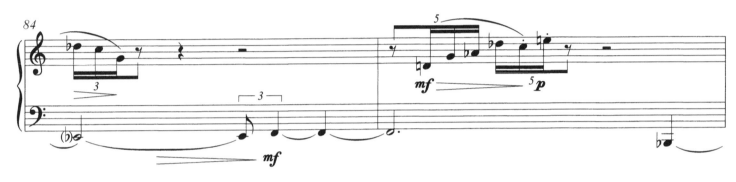

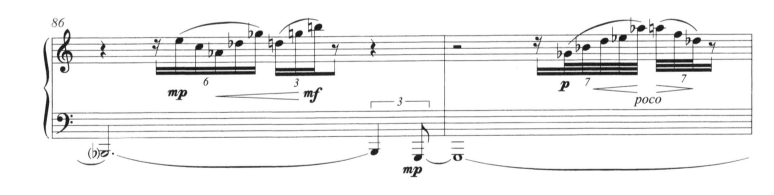

*To Robert Helps*

# Ballad in Yellow
(*after Lorca*)

DAVID DEL TREDICI
(1997)

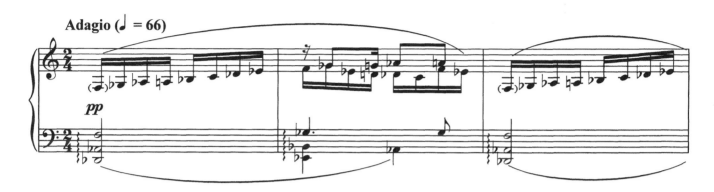

a tempo

62

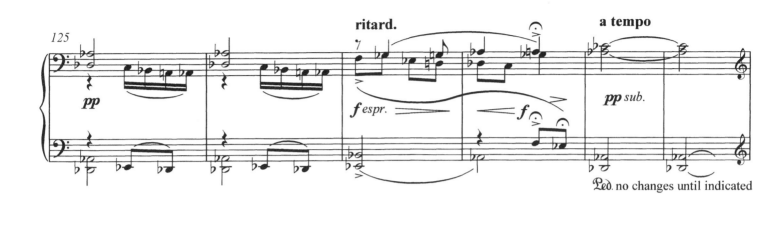

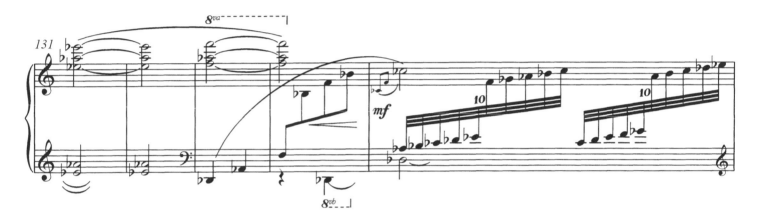

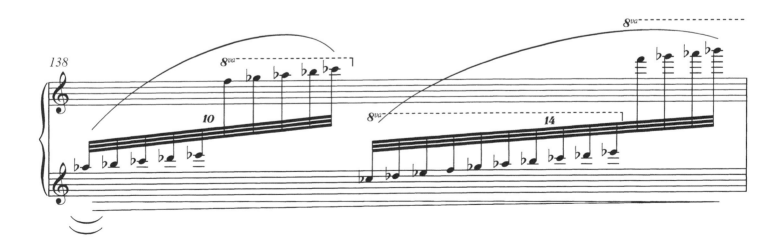

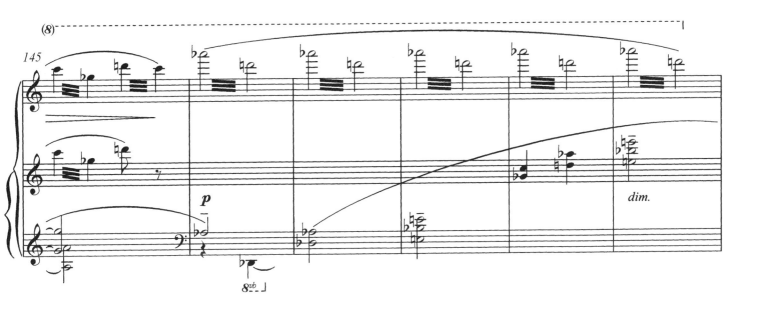

6/22/97 Yaddo,
Saratoga Springs, NY

*For Leo Smit*

# Four Piano Blues

## 1

AARON COPLAND
(1926-48)

1947

*For Andor Foldes*
2

**Soft and languid** ( ♩ = 108)

mark the bass melody

1934

*For William Kapell*

3

Muted and sensuous (♩ = 66)

1948

*For John Kirkpatrick*

4

1948

*for John Browning*

# Prelude No. 2
from *Twenty-Four Preludes*

RICHARD CUMMING
(1966)

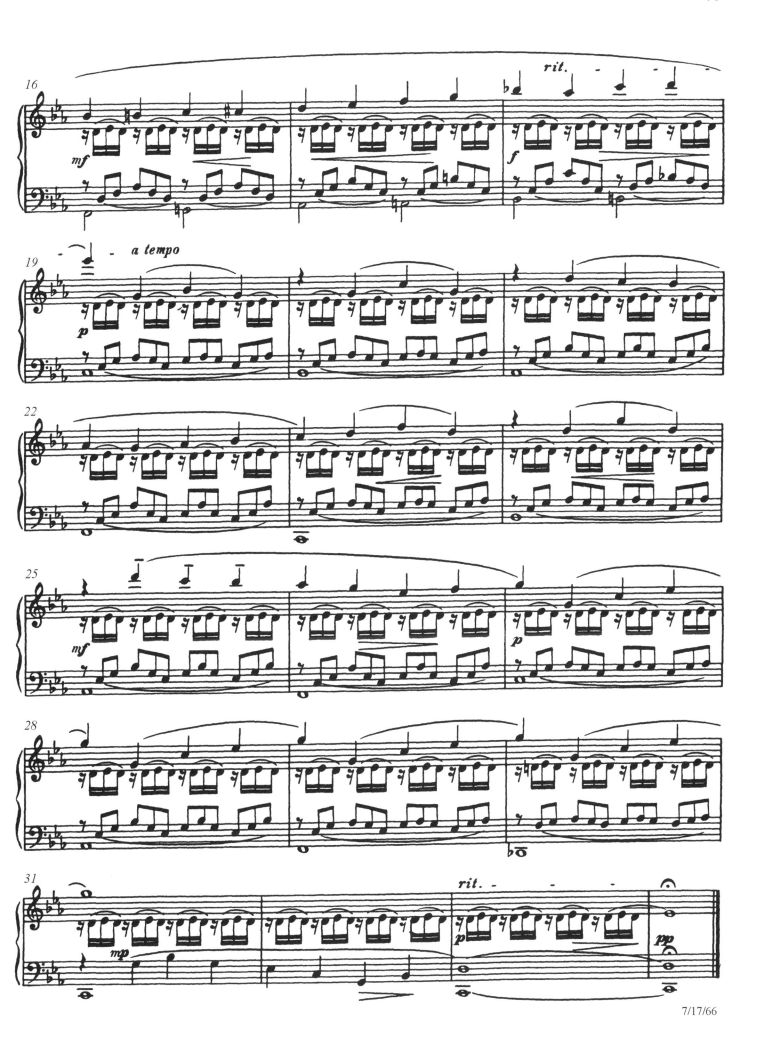

*for John Browning*

# Prelude No. 9
### from *Twenty-Four Preludes*

RICHARD CUMMING
(1969)

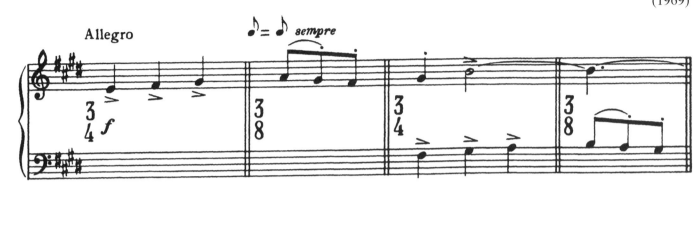

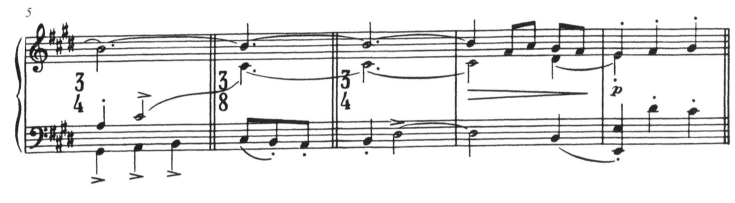

*for John Browning*

# Prelude No. 11

from *Twenty-Four Preludes*

RICHARD CUMMING
(1966)

*for John Browning*

# Prelude No. 24

from *Twenty-Four Preludes*

RICHARD CUMMING
(1967)

82

*For Evlyn Howard-Jones*

# Five Piano Pieces
## I. Mazurka

FREDERICK DELIUS
(1923)

*For Yvonne O'Neill*
## II. Waltz

(1923)

*For Evlyn Howard-Jones*

## III. Waltz

Croissy 1891
(finished at Grez sur Loing 1922)

# IV. Lullaby
## for a modern baby

(1922)

## V. Toccata

# Fantasia

BENJAMIN LEES
(1954)

100

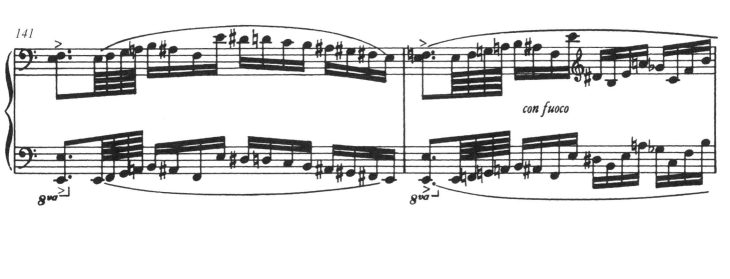

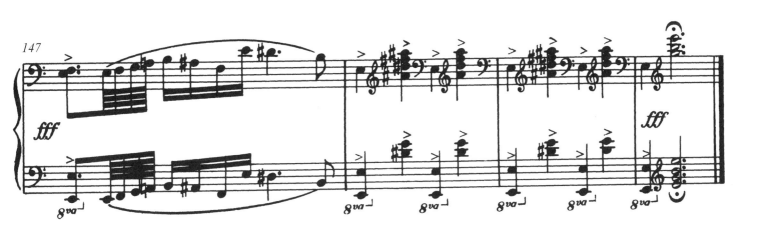

# Pequeña Danza

from the ballet *Estancia*, Op. 8

ALBERTO GINASTERA
(1941)

*for my children Alex and Georgina*

# Rondo
## on Argentine children's folk-tunes, Op. 19

ALBERTO GINASTERA
(1947)

*a Rudolf Firkusny*

# Suite de danzas criollas
## Op. 15

### I.

ALBERTO GINASTERA
(1946, rev. 1956)

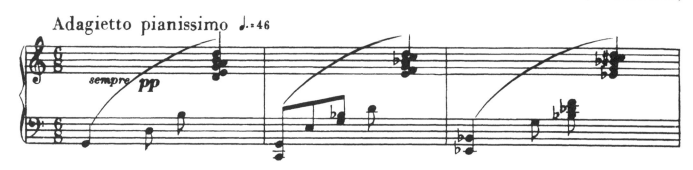

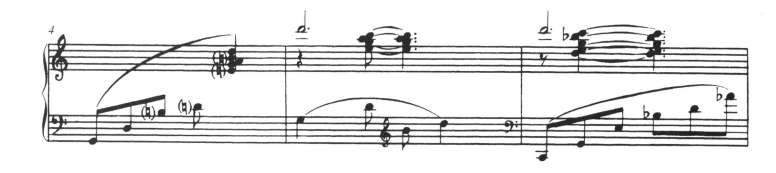

114

II.

Allegro rustico ♩.=126

*Con la palma de la mano.*
*) Ossia:  Avec la paume.
*With the palm of the hand.*

III.

## IV.

V.

Coda

# Intermezzo

Andenken an Poul Rovsing Olsen

HENRYK MIKOŁAJ GÓRECKI
(1990)

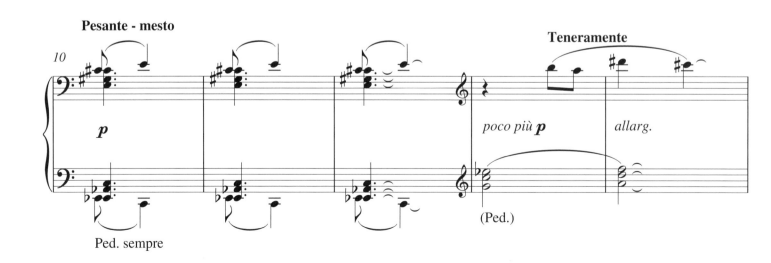

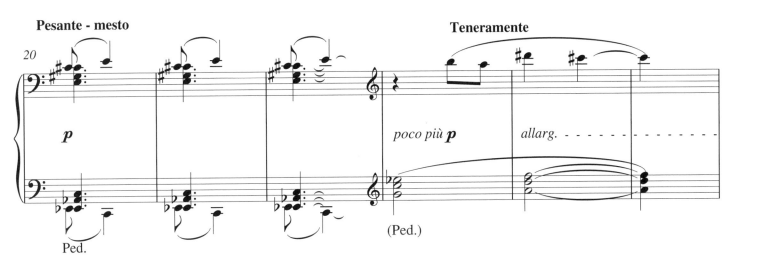

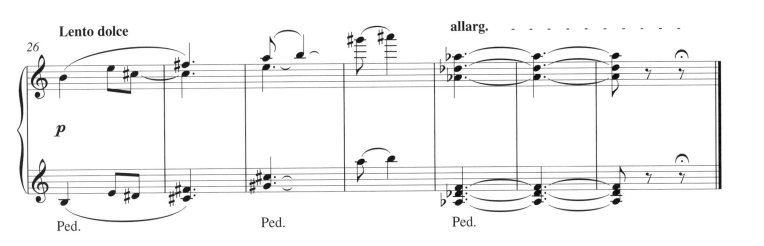

# Rhapsody

JOHN IRELAND
(1915)

*for Llyr Williams*

# Madog

KARL JENKINS
(2009)

**Moto perpetuo – in strict time**  ♩ = 236–240

# Russian Rag

ELENA KATS-CHERNIN
(1996)

**Dreamy, with rubato**

♩ = 88

*(molto Ped.)*

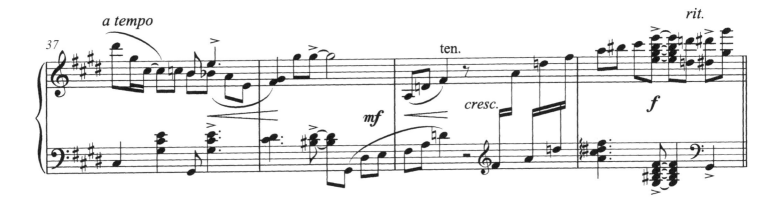

**Livelier** ♩ = 88

January 1996, Coogee

*for Norma Marschke*

# Combination Rag

ELENA KATS-CHERNIN
(1999)

Ped. ⎯⎯⎯⎯⎤ Ped. ⎯⎯⎯⎤ Ped. ⎯⎯⎯⎤ Ped. sim.

156

Più mosso

16 June 1999, 4:00 PM, Coogee

# Etude in A

from *Etudes and Polkas, Book 1*

BOHUSLAV MARTINŮ
(1945)

164

# Polka in A

from *Etudes and Polkas, Book 1*

BOHUSLAV MARTINŮ
(1945)

170

August 28, 1945
S. Orleans, Mass.

# Etude in F

from *Etudes and Polkas, Book 2*

BOHUSLAV MARTINŮ
(1945)

*To Winifred Johnstone*

# Polka in A
from *Etudes and Polkas, Book 3*

BOHUSLAV MARTINŮ
(1945)

# Song & Dance

NED ROREM
(1986)

Nantucket & New York City
12-18 October, 1986

*Commissioned by the Iitti Music Festival*
*Dedicated to Laura Mikkola*

# Passionale

EINOJUHANI RAUTAVAARA
(2003)

\* The x sign after a note extends its duration by a quarter

*To my wife*

# Serenade in A

Edited by
SOULIMA STRAVINSKY

IGOR STRAVINSKY
(1925)

Hymn

* All trills start on the note

* Depress without striking

Romanza

* Release key half way while retaining vibration

* All grace-notes before the beat

* Depress without striking

# Rondoletto

* Depress without striking

## Cadenza Finale

# Travelling in Spain: Alice Woodfin Branlière

from *Thirteen Portraits*

VIRGIL THOMSON
(1929)

Paris, October 24, 1929

# Invention: Theodate Johnson Busy and Resting

from *Thirteen Portraits*

VIRGIL THOMSON
(1940)

216

Paris, April 29, 1940